Grief Touched the Sky at Night

POEMS BY

Gloria Mindock

Glass Lyre Press

Copyright © 2023 Gloria Mindock
Paperback ISBN: 979-8-9885737-3-9

All rights reserved: Except for the purpose of quoting brief passages for review, no part of this book may be reproduced or transmitted in any form or by any means, electronic or mechanical, including photocopying, recording, or by any information storage and retrieval system, without permission in writing from the publisher.

Design & Layout: Steven Asmussen
Cover Photo: Natalia Zhurminskaya

Glass Lyre Press, LLC
P.O. Box 2693
Glenview, IL 60025
www.GlassLyrePress.com

Books by Gloria Mindock

ASH
Pepeo/ASH, Translated into the Serbian by Milutin Djurickovic
Whiteness of Bone
I Wish Francisco Franco Would Love Me
La Porțile Raiului/At the Heavens Gate, Translated into the Romanian by Flavia Cosma
Nothing Divine Here
Blood Soaked Dresses

Chapbooks
Pleasure Trout
Oh Angel
Doppelganger

Plays
Odd Bones

Grief Touched the Sky at Night

For Svetoslav Nahum

Contents

Decomposition

First Day of War	1
The Blindfold	2
Bandages	3
Bells of Kyiv	4
Bruised	5
Another Day in War	6
Numb	7
Playtime	8
Memory	9
The Threat	10
Fog	11
The Map	12
де моя мама	13
Blue Skies and Sunflowers	14
Boots	15
Bucha	16
Bullseye	17
Putin	18
You	19

BEFORE WAR

Before War	23
Belief	24
Birds	25
Fear	26
Good-bye	27
Noise	28
Rain	29
Song	30
Surface	31
The Chapel	32
Exceeding	33
Clear	34
Don't You	35
The Faucet	36
Perfection	37
Disloyalty	38
Disaster	39
The Silence	40
Stalking	41
Shy	42
Requiem	43
I Don't Mourn	44
Gone	45
Fake	46
Dreams	47

ANESTHESIA

Crows	51
Loss	52
One Day in Ukraine	53
Earth	54
Sometimes	55
Carrying	56
Peace	57
Stone	58
My Last Moments	59
Regret	60
Winding Road	61
Apocalypse	62
Acknowledgments	65
About the Author	69
Author's Note	71

Decomposition

First Day of War

I ran down twenty-one flights of stairs
to find myself
sitting under a tree
branches sheltering me from grief
The wind blowing it somewhere…

The Blindfold

Blindfold me so I don't see the damage,
the dead bodies, or blood on the ground.

Wrap the blindfold tightly around my eyes so
I don't see the Russian tanks.

Puncture my ears so I don't hear the sirens that
a missile is coming.

Tie my hands together so I can't take
a life. God would not want me to do this.

Bind my legs so I won't run and flee
from my home.

Stop my heart from feeling loss, sadness
and grief before it overwhelms me.

The soldiers are killing my family and friends.
Slitting their throats and burning them. I know this.

Remove my blindfold
Untie my hands
Give me my hearing back
Give me a weapon.

Bandages

In a Russian prison, she could
hear the cries of Ukrainian men being raped.
She was pregnant. Her husband did not know.
All she wanted was her baby to be born in Ukraine.
Speaking to her stomach, urging, Wait little one.
In a prisoner exchange, her baby was born in Ukraine.

Another woman, so brutalized
She was not sure she would live,
yet she's ready to fight again.
Still, she did not want to leave home:
Bombed out shell.
Dried blood in the dirt.
Wreckage like abstract art.
A boot in the road filled with flowers.
Someone mourning a life. Mourning their life.

In some villages, every heart stopped beating at once.
Can a village survive supported by the beating hearts of only two?
Yet the women carry on in the footprints stretched out before them.
walking the same path,
breathing a different story for a free Ukraine.

Bells of Kyiv

The churches are empty,
half standing,
no bells to ring.

In the wreckage,
lays a cross no one
has touched.

Jesus lays there.
Broken.

Is there a meaning to this?
Will he rise again
in this country?

Someone will pick him up,
carry him in their arms,
kiss the cross he is on.

Everyone needs to be protected,
to be loved.
Someone else will find his hand.
No nails binding the freedom
we all need.

Bruised

Body, broken

What is to become of us in
this sweeping wind?

Can missiles be blown away?
A storm that stops corpses

My newborn is dead
Crouched in a basement,
no pill to kill the pain for me

My family, in makeshift graves.

At midnight, I hear my baby crying,
but she is gone to where there
is no sin.

Another Day in War

Mankind has weapons to kill.
In a few seconds, millions can be wiped out.

Strollers in the center of town showing
the children who are gone.
Families losing family.
No home to go back to.
Bullet holes left where there once was life.

Neighboring countries open their arms,
graves too are open…
So many weeping for the losses.

In Russia, it will snow forever.
A penance from any melting.
The ice, hard.

Many are leaving.

Yesterday, I took the hand of my Ukrainian friend and
Russian friend, we danced for the stars
to light the way…

Numb

War is bursting.
Fate is always death.
Flames move from building to building.
Bodies scorched.
The landscape is caught in the language
of the enemy.

Nothing seems real.
A bewildered population picks up
guns, praying for some magic to happen.

Is this a dream?
Pain numbed by gunfire—
a crucifixion of bullets.
A makeshift cemetery where the bodies fall.

It is obvious, this decomposing won't stop.
Bandages won't help.
The worm will find its way.

Playtime

Political parties will not end this war.
People protest for a paradise…
a place where there are no bullets ripping bodies apart.
As a young girl, I see it all—
It haunts me…
an inheritance I have no choice over.

Each night, before I go to sleep, I pray for quiet.
I can never play with dolls.
My childhood is soaked with blood.
The stains are what I play with.
Swirling the red to make stick figures.
Pretending it's my parents to take care of me.

Today, I put on the prettiest dress I have—
wait for this camouflage
to take me elsewhere.

Memory

I cannot open my mouth.
It is taped shut.
My hands tied behind my back, feet in chains,
hurting my ankles, digging into skin, bone, cutting…

The sky is red.
The rivers are red.
My heart is not.

The bombs go off.
I hear them getting closer and closer.
So loud, hurts my ears, they ring…
I cannot hear my thoughts…

Crying, scared, a senseless death awaits—
Why am I in this world at all?

The moon inspects the earth—
does not like what it sees…
Murder, witnessed with its pale brightness…

I did not want to be erased like this.
Another number, a body, with no hope visible…
I bleed soundless.

The Threat

Why must we die in our own country, if another country can help us live? Let us go! No need to watch us from the window so closely. We shut our blinds to an obscure lightness and need no residence with your death schedule. Our pictures will not be put on a wall for remembrance. A journey up the stairs would be nice, emerging us from the depths that threatened us with coffins.

Fog

It is foggy, clouds nourishing
the ground, sky.
There is something about the way
clouds layer like blankets.

In your country, I would like to think
you are warm, have food
to keep you alive.

It has now become a ritual, this suffering,
day and night missiles strike,
people are shot by the enemy,
dead bodies on the ground.

I want the fog to hide you, lift you up,
take you to a new place, or take the soldiers away,
giving ground back,
where all of Ukraine can live once again.
All that is destroyed
is reborn again.

The Map

Sadness will not desert us.
This country fights but will not disappear.
I would like to paint a special canvas
for you to hang on your wall, but I can't.

There is no food to feed the many
tongues of need.
This territory is bombed flat.
Many fled but some did not.
Their heart is buried deep in this soil.
No amount of death will make it less.

They look tattered but are brave.
Their skin blossoms into Sunflowers daily.
Aiming towards the sun.
Facing beauty of the light in a dark hell.

On a map of the country, there
is only destruction seen.
The people are proud raising their arms
to take land back.
A gesture of existence on the battlefront,
they are heroes fighting the occupied cities
collapsing the fangs which try to bite down.

ДЕ МОЯ МАМА

Where is my mama?
Sorry, she is not at home

Where is my daddy?
With the soldiers

Where are my brothers?
In mass graves

Where is my sister?
In a Russian prison

Where am I?
Hiding.

Where am I?
In rumble

Where am I?
Alone

Blue Skies and Sunflowers

Watching a country crumble hurts.
Eyes sad, as people lay dead.
All the sunflowers drenched in blood.
Do the petals throb?
It is said that plants talk to one another.
What they must think.

In one town, the crows fly down and
kiss the bodies.
Maybe I dreamt this…

Is it wrong to wish him dead?

Grief touches the black sky at night,
the blue in daylight.
The ground decayed with pieces of life.
Too much bombardment.
Too much hate.

Ukraine fights for freedom.
Heroes up against a cruel dance.
Bombed buildings, hospitals, roads, and existence
laying on the ground
Uncertain, if they have much longer.

Weep in unison, dear people.
We are weeping with you…

Boots

My boots are dirty
but not from dirt.

My boots are heavy
but not from weight

My boots are untied
but not from neglect

My boots are on the road
I did not take them off

My boots are worn by someone else
I did not give

My body is naked
I did not remove my clothes

My dignity remains
while the dirt covers me

I love my country.
I love my country.

I am Ukraine.

Bucha

A tragedy
The sky turned red
Blood
The Russian soldiers fed

With force, with guns
A village now hostage
They rounded up who they could
Pulling them out of their houses
Hands tied behind backs

Screams, shots, rape, brutality
Families watched their loved ones
Murdered

HORROR

The world cries with hearts broken
But does not help
Sends weapons only
Making victims of all of us

Souls of the deceased will never rest
Until freedom is achieved
The broken land rejoined

Standing with Ukraine
The colors of your flag raised
Blend in with the sky
Sunflowers wilted
But soon will bloom
As evil is defeated

Bucha, we love you

Bullseye

I stand in the middle of town.
A bullseye for the missile.

Let me feel some control.
Give me a gun to hold.

I say good-bye.

Farewell, to a life I loved.
Destroyed.

Hope is something I need.

Yellow sunflowers
blow in the dust.

I know it is time.
Waiting…

Putin

A golden room to sit in.

What sort of others sit there?
In chairs so soft, they drown in the cushions.
Only their heads sticking out.
A David Lynch image, dissolving into
the floor, melting words harsh and cold like
the marble floor they land on.

Once Man roamed the earth
looking for worms.
Putin ate them so Man could not find any.
After years, Man finally gave up.
Moved on to looking for ants.
There were so many.
Man would collect and sneak
them back into the offices of Putin
to watch them all squirm.

It was Man's way of fighting back
quietly, yet disarming.

You

There is a key to the sky Putin and you
don't have it.
You will see nothing but black
for the rest of your life.
Pay, you little depressed repulsive man!

Drop down into this atmosphere and whistle
as they close your coffin lid.
Magnification of a dark suit for a nothingness

Before War

Before War

Sadness arrives late morning.
I expected it.
My only solace is at 1:00 AM
when all the houses are quiet, no car noise
on the street, stars bright, and a
calmness in the air.

Happiness touches my skin in the moonlight.
Energized, I know I should be asleep.

Is there a way to switch hours?
Wake up happy and go to bed sad.
Sleep it off like a drunk each night.

Another day, an unknown.
The thankfulness of being alive
continuously urges me to breathe.

Belief

Some people believe in Angels,
some don't.
Everyone has to believe in something!
If not this, then what?

Sometimes, there are too many
cracks not fixed.
Even in the deepest part of the heart,
there is beating.
Sometimes just not evident.

It is true, all you have to do is
flood the dark with light?

Birds

All birds fly. Beautifully…
My eyes watch them every morning at 5:30.
What eternal secrets can they share?

When evening arrives, I leave my tears.
In the morning, they are picked up by the birds.
They carry my thoughts into the air.
Flapping their wings as if to explain to the world
what I gave them. Trying to tell my story.

One day, five landed on my arm trying to tell me something.
Then, flew away into the clouds.
There is no line between us.
Only an understanding that we all must
share a branch, perch…

The birds gave me their song, and kept
my bleeding for the infinite.

Fear

The unknown is waiting
to take me into the air.
Those gone, gather around me

What to expect?
I do not know.
If I stay on earth, a bomb or a bullet will find me.

I fear pain

With hands clasped together,
my soul molds into the universe…
A space where everything drifts
into a new black.

Good-bye

I always liked getting lost in cornfields.
You never could find me.
The stalks bothered my skin so stayed
hidden only for a little while.

Miles and miles of corn, sticking up
from flatness, reaching for the sky.
You could never understand my love for this.

So many bad storms.
Lightning scaring the horses.
They break loose and run
in the field.
Appreciating freedom like me
as we swallow the sky.

Noise

I look through the darkness but see nothing.
Blackness lets my imagination erupt—
multiplying…

When a noise is heard,
its power overwhelms me.
Where is it coming from?

Listening could become a habit.
Difficult to break.
I want quiet to surface in
this night air.

Resting my hands on my bed,
rocking myself to sleep…
I nestle within.

Rain

The day is cloudy.
Rain dripping off the branches of trees,
soaking the ground.
The flowers bloom like they do every year.

It was yesterday, darkness was seen.
Flames from missiles striking so many buildings.
Neighbors crying for help.
Some dying before they were reached.

Now the walls are bare, stained with blood.
Grief overflows from my heart.
It does not matter how many times the sky changes color.

The clouds will drift forever.
Morning never comes again.

When the night is back to normal, I will
be back to a home I love, with a voice
defying all the loss, a depth bearing no end,
a void interconnected with death.

Song

There is a sadness in the air—
heaviness pressing down on bones,
cracking them—
a mourning over the world.

We know what it means
saying good-bye to the ground where
we think you are.

Wounded
We weep silently
hearing machine guns in the distance...
A horizon of blood

Being one with the earth,
when it is our time to be buried,
who will follow when war breaks out?
A never-ending orchard
of flowers.

Surface

Daylight decodes this moment.
It is the Holy Grail for life.

There is nothingness, silence,
restlessness, dark fighting for control.

My heart dances, stops.
Dances, dreams.
Dances, spins.

Whatever is to come
will be delivered
spinning into certainty

I used to think that I felt
I was wrong

coldness like steel, there is
no breaking.
My surface is forming a barrier
where I flourish in the void.

The Chapel

So many Icons to look at.
Eyes go from one to another.
ceilings of gold—

If I can't see everything
is my faith enough?

People are talking in The Sistine Chapel!
How could they?
It made me dizzy seeing the painting.

Someone told the people to shut up.
They kept disregarding the sacred.

The two hands did not strike
their mouths.
No wrath from the ceiling.
Some of us cried tears
in our own silence.

The talkers missed a most
important message.
How could they?

---

*Some of the most beautiful and old churches in Ukraine have been destroyed. Masterpieces of beauty. This poem is included in this collection in honor of the Orthodox churches in Ukraine. I ask the same question to the Russian soldiers as the people talking in the Sistine Chapel: How could they?

Exceeding

No one lives like I do
No freedom, just flames
Days of putting defeat in a vase

I am wishing for a miracle
Remember, you always see me falling off ladders
The devil lives in all the wounds

I do not know where my son is buried
Did he die slowly or quickly?
These thoughts are playing endlessly.

Tears fall from eyes in a trance
Sleep is in rations

Give me a shirt with words so
I do not have to speak anymore
There is nothing left to say
The moon still shines

There is no loss of light
Only a dimness attaching itself to me

Clear

There is no fear in not knowing.
Strength comes from moments
here and there.

Ash comes from the results
of an explosion—
pieces of life all over.

It all is thrown away.
You can start over,
build up again as the
sky witnesses your being.

The blue sky clear of any dust.

Don't You

Don't you ever want to stop the vowels
from coming out of your mouth?
Even on this fall day with leaves dropping off trees,
don't you want to step on them, hear the crunch?

Don't you want to be in silence just for a little bit?
Feel the breeze on skin?

Out of my mouth come consonants you never hear.
Ignored, I try to speak louder so you will.
Something is missing in our lives
where the vowels and consonants don't connect.

I turned a corner in life to find beauty in trees.
Falling like leaves into long sentences.
Whereas you have laryngitis, missing the bright colors—
the sound of air.

It is too late for you.
It's apparent, you can only be slurs
buried into the earth.

The Faucet

The faucet is dripping.
I cup my hand to drink a few drops.
It is not enough.
My throat is dry and the distance between
dry and wet is enormous.

How many times I have taken advantage of
thinking things will always be ok.
In the next room a family hides like me.
When are we ever safe?

My mouth is stuffed with death, waiting
for the blast.
With regret, I open the window for air but
only smoke seeps in.

I can't breathe.
This is my final thought until tomorrow…
I will try again to drink from the few
things life still offers.

Perfection

I am drawn to perfection,
so explain how to end war.
Damp graves, heavy bones,
there is no way not to walk past.

At home, I pray to the Saints.
The icons hanging on the wall.
Who are they?
I don't know but love the images.

The silence is scary.
Are the Saints preparing
my heart for bullets?

Blessing myself with holy water,
bullets hit point blank.
Stars pull me toward them.
As this happens, the war expands
soaking the land with blood.

You should have prayed,
Stuck your hands in the Black Sea for
non-existent currents.

At this hour of incense, violence will hold tight.
Let a drop of rain hit your lip.
It will be your last Holy Communion.

Disloyalty

Disloyalty came easy—
an inherited present.
The family deputizing the
body with abandonment.
Thoughts of love, dead.

Hands, now terminal.
Grabbing on to something but nothing is there.
Eyes refrain from looking into the sky.

It is no use, existence is
beyond light, crawling on an
endless merry-go-round.

Disaster

I suffer many woes,
not serene but impossible.
Always on the edge,
crashing into you,
plunging with force
for your heart to welcome
my disaster.

My life floats in fragments—
I try to grab them.
You, absent.
Me, surrendering to my fate.

No tears, only clouds breezing by
chauffeuring me away, where I
dream of you, lips quivering,
for a moment in the past.

The Silence

There is so much grief
in the sky weighing its
blue on me.
Pausing and stunned, I go
and sit beneath a tree.
Its branches ache for me
dropping leaves of sorrow.

How many dead people watch
my body on the grass?
It's soft against my clothes.
A comfort surrounding me.

Feeling lost, empty, a bird
flies overhead as I stand.
I don't need to tell you what it did.
A reminder that life can be low.

Walking, I explode into life with a yearning
to live one more day…
for a heart that no longer beats.

That tree understood.
It was telling me,
we all have sorrow.

Stalking

If it were left to me,
I would not recognize you.
No matter that you are every place I go.

You can't follow me forever.

It could be possible for you to notice someone else.
Not at all like me.
Perhaps sooner or later amnesia will take over.
None of this matters.

Your absence would be nice
Back to peaceful days, sleep,
without waking with all these words in my head or
nightmares on a skewer burning…

Shy

Living in resistance where words
don't feel shy. If not heard,
they will only float
in the abyss…

My life remains doubtful to
the whims of others.
Pain has become a habit of enduring.
The sign of the cross, a ritual of images,
prayers of rain.

Buildings fall around me.
Concrete so impatient, it has
to crumble.
Death has entered this city.

This waiting is forever.
Taking cover, not knowing
how much longer I have,
my only certainty is the sirens,
howling like wind in my ears.

Flooded by tears, my body
drowns in weariness,
this moment, this time.
A vacuum of sadness…
Grief accompanies me into infinity
for the last rays of light.

Requiem

In this city, we all get struck by cars.
Body parts flying unable to reconnect.
No thoughts of tomorrow.

Pardon this Amen
each time you see me.
The color I wear is black—
consequences of embracing life.

My descent into the unknown
is a daily event.
Death confronts me at every turn.
Ignoring it is what I do.

I try to be normal, but spend my time
hiding in everyone's breath.

I Don't Mourn

I mourn what I throw away,
old paintings, photographs, objects, writings—
Each thing drifts in the wind,
trying to stick to life but can't.

Is this me too?
trying to hang on—
No one has the same memories—
same things in possession.
Must I give all this up?

Ignore me, I don't mourn.
Best to close down.
Shut my eyes tight until
darkness is my fate.

I can have little funerals daily as
I pitch out life.
This way, you will never own me.
You don't want to anyway.
Junk to you.

From the grave, hope my things
will visit me.
I don't want to be alone.
Maybe you will sit by stone and talk.
Carrying in your pocket your favorite thing of mine.

Gone

The rain hits my skin
washing away my heart.
Down the street it floats,
finally going down the sewer drain.

It is still beating as it stays afloat,
doesn't drown.
See, no matter how you hoped,
I still survive.

Years ago, things were nice between us.
Now that I am gone,
I make my own formations in the air.
To this day, I do not miss you.

In the distance, you stay motionless.
I kept your secrets but now, remember
none of them.

Going about my life, I am not mournful.
I go with new love,
tenderly,
we look after one another
dissolving each other into our mouths.

Fake

I haven't seen you in years.
You were only an image, fading…

Your heart beats for fame.
Failure attached to you.
I did not see it.
It was all there but buried.

I tore up our photos in the trunk.

Memories like dreams are forgotten.
Disintegrating into the air.
Just breezes going by
not stopping on skin.

Dreams

The light clings to the glass reflecting your eyes.
Is it too late to close them? See darkness for awhile…
There is no map to help for where to go.
Life passes quickly like a parade.
Music weaves in and out. A gift in this existence.
It plays while spectators clap and cheer.
No matter what happens, the moonlight is calm.
Gives you a touch of flight.

Hold on to your dreams.
You can unwrap them any time.
Look outside and they are in the breeze,
floating in the air, wanting to fall into
your breath nightly.

ANESTHESIA

Crows

The crows are perched on the
back fence, warning me of death
Graceful in their waiting like my
mother and her mother before her

After death, the birds bring gifts
to help with mourning, when life is gone
The crows know that everything ends
up in the abyss

Guarding the transition, the abandoning
of earth, through all the grief,
memories scatter in the grass as I
walk and they chatter

Give me my brothers back, my mom—
to live an infinite life among us
Images returning before they disappear
once more
A crossroad where we all connect
feeling the same air

Loss

Today, I threw myself
into the garbage.
Bits of me, memories…

It all will end in the trash anyway.
I must be the one to say good-bye.
Send it all on a journey to the incinerator.

I am mourning the pieces of me
burning
like I was never here.

Maybe you will hear me
crying for all I let go.

One Day in Ukraine

Raking the fallen leaves into a pile,
I look forward to jumping in,
throwing them up into the air.

Stepping on them, hearing the crunch,
the sound pushes crispness into the ground.
They nestle with the earth,
find soil in a different way.

This always makes me think of you—
where you are.
Do you see the colors as they
change and fall?
They almost match your uniform.

Will you be watching me as I age and decline
until I am in the earth?
Is there someone who will visit me?

Will you find me as I wait?

Earth

The earth is up to it again,
rotating into darkness.
No memory of daylight

The sea opens its mouth.
Waves crash on the shore...

Darkness climbs into the water.
It is always slippery.
The heart knows the boundaries of both.

There is always another side to things.
Sometimes we belong to each,
not sure what direction to take

Everyone is wet and cold.
Dryness will not happen without a towel.
Sometimes, you have to approach things differently.
Fall in love with the edge.

Sometimes

Sometimes, even the wind gets tired.
Maybe today it doesn't want to blow.
Maybe today the earth would like to stop spinning.
Gravity would like to let go.

Imagine everything drifting into space—
people and objects not mattering anymore.
A stampede of floating humans surrounded by junk.

Sometimes I like to forget all wars.
Maybe someday they will stop.
There will be no buttons to push,
no nuclear missiles to end the earth.

Maybe someday I will smile again and the warm
air will be just warm, no fire to burn us to ash.

Maybe someday I will see you again,
standing in your kitchen with a drink
not minding the darkness around us

The dark, a dream, that awakened us.
Reality is something we don't want,
no light calling on our hearts to fix things.
Maybe sometimes, it feels good to forget…

Carrying

What is it about destruction that is
so easy but creating takes longer

What is it about the sun beating on skin
making you feel warm then the cold takes it away

The ashes are blown to infinity
wind carrying them continent to continent

What is this all about
memory that won't let go.

Peace

The dead have gray skin.
Ashes fall on them today.
Church bells ring dreamily as the survivors weep.

Life is empty, hollow.
Wind ceases.
The world forgets this place.

Witness the remains beneath us
Today, dirt is thrown on bodies.
Fragments of life lost mix with the
blood of the innocent

Stone

It is never over—
the dying, one after another.
A procession like words on a page,
used continuously.
Gravestones firm on the ground.
It is the only time you can be secure.
Take a stance on the ground.

The weeds will no longer make you itch.
Your heart will not bleed from sadness.
Belongings all gone taking shelter somewhere.
The people you know will be gone soon,
if not already.

Take comfort like me.
There will always be chaos, no
matter where you are.
But once in the coffin, rest.

Roots reach for the dirt,
bones grab for texture.
An object only, collected on earth,
trying to find a place among stones.
Once again, you want to be heard.

You want to be remembered each time
the wind hits the face of the living.

My Last Moments

In hiding. Blending in with the walls.
Complete darkness, no panic.
Night explosions ruin my solitude.

One blast after another.
The doves are in the trash.
I wanted a life but have none.
No shoes or a place to go.
I sit and entertain myself.
Sneaking a peek out the window.

I dream of a beautiful breeze touching
my face. The moon gives me comfort.
All I hear are heavy boots coming for me.

When I was a little girl, I thought the world was
a beautiful place. I was wrong.
I can smell the stench of dead bodies.
Soon, I will be among them.

Aren't we all waiting for the slaughter?
We are animals, sharp teeth baring…
There is no Eden, only this godforsaken place.
Lives destroyed. Mine destroyed, thrown away.
We all are thrown away, bodies with
hearts cut out by the enemy, rotting in a pile,
mangled.

Regret

I give you love letters to
infiltrate your invalid body.
You will rise to worship
a new me.

My throat reaches another level.

Threaten / Press you / Save /
Destroy.

Your heart is
of a sterile army
fighting to kill clear skies.

I swallow our relationship
but you only choke.

Winding Road

Where does this road end,
I think as I wander piecing
my life together.
But I think it's too late.

It can't be reunited.
If I shoot will you live?
I won't wrap your wounds.

Blood seeps out one way
or another
leaving everything dry.
I am just going to stand here
and watch for the red puddle
to form on the ground.

The clouds look unhappy making a noise.

Apocalypse

Once upon a time, earth was a beautiful place.
Now, this is only a fairytale dreamt about, wished for…

Our planet is broken, air is becoming obsolete.
All life, dying—
We now play connect the dots to everything we've done,
saying we must change.
It is too late. Wolf cried too many times.

Plastic, mercury, garbage, and oil in the oceans, I heard it on the news
Sewage, garbage in rivers, seen this
Pollution, emissions and holes in the ozone layer, breathe
Trees in forests cut down, no home for wildlife, stumps everywhere
Forest fires, see the flames, smell the smoke
Drought, no water, cracked earth
Pesticides, poison just for you
GMO, mutants
Cell phones, oh brain dead, brain dead, Electromagnetic Radiation
Electricity Towers, my hair is sticking straight up, cows dead in fields
Storms, bomb cyclones, hurricanes, tornadoes, go for a ride
Radioactivity, nuclear power waste, I'm glowing
Gravity pull, bye-bye earth
Warheads ready to strike, poof

Beauty, fading. A memory disappearing…
A bare planet spinning in the universe.
There is no future for the generations to come.

No history of existence.

This planet will break into pieces, thanks for mining
end up in a black hole.
No evidence of being, chemicals embalmed us

Man is leaving himself impassioned with dust.
We are dirt in more ways than one.
No more sweeping it under the rug, how cliche
a tumor in the head causes turning towards Mars, sick bastards
and once that is destroyed, yeah, keep going

Stupid man, you are gone—
Apocalypse Baby!

"The sun ain't gonna shine anymore…"

Acknowledgments

Constellations: A Journal of Poetry and Fiction, "Perfection," "Blue Skies and Sunflowers," "Another Day in War"

Contemporary Dialogues, Macedonian Science Society, "Crows," "Bandages,B" "Bullseye," "Bucha," "The Faucet," translated into the Macedonian by Daniela Andonovska-Trajkovska

En la Masmédula, Mexico, Falso (Fake), Pérdida (Loss), and El Silencio (The Silence), translated into the Spanish by Mariela Cordero

Growth: Journal of Literature, Culture, & Art, "Noise" and "The Blindfold" translated into the Macedonian by Daniela Andonovaska-Trajkovska

Ibbetson Street, "Apocalypse," "The Blindfold," and "Bandages"

International Poetry Anthology, "Bells of Kyiv"

JazzKedisi, "Disaster," translated into Turkish by Erkut Tokman

KGB Lit, "Noise" and "Stalking"

Lily Poetry Review of Books, "Crows"

Live Nude Poems, "Bucha"

Muddy River Poetry Review, "Stone," "The Faucet," "Don't You," "My Last Moments," "Gone," "Dreams," "Disloyalty," and "Birds"

OPA, "Playtime," "Memory," and "The Threat"

POÉMAME: revista abierta de poesia, Spain, un dia en ucrania (One Day in Ukraine), Falso (Fake), Pérdida (Loss), translated into the Spanish by Mariela Cordero

Rye Whiskey Review, "The Map"

Setu: A Bilingual Journal of Literature - Western Voices, "Sometimes," "Bruised," "Rain," "Shy," "Fog," and "Loss"

Somerville Times, The Lyrical, "Putin"

Sunflowers: Ukrainian Poems on War, Resistance, Hope, and Peace, "Numb"

The Crossroads, "Carrying"

The James Dickey Review, "Earth" and "Surface"

Veritas Review, "Requiem," "Song," "Bullseye," "Exceeding," "The Chapel," "Good-bye," "Clear," "Belief"

World of Poetry and American Poets, "Before War"

∽

Thank you to Ami Kaye for believing in my work, the continuous support, and friendship throughout the years. Thank you to Steve Asmussen for all you do. You are amazing! I am so grateful to you and all the Glass Lyre Press staff.

A heartfelt thank you to my friends Karen Friedland and Renuka Raghavan who workshopped many of these poems in our group. You both are the greatest and always there for me!

A special thanks goes out to friends Catherine Sasanov, Susan Tepper, and Joy Martin for suggestions given on some of these poems.

I am so grateful to Svet DiNahum, Eric Pankey and Vasyl Makhno for writing such incredible blurbs.

A very special thank you to Natalia Zhurminskaya for giving me permission to use her photo taken in Crimea for my cover. It is so perfect and exactly what I wanted. Thanks to Svet DiNahum for referring her to me.

Thanks so much to Rich Feinberg for proofing. I cannot thank you enough for your help!

There are so many editors of journals who published many of these poems. I am forever grateful to you for giving my poems a home. They are: Nina Rubinstein Alonso, Mariela Cordero, Daniela Andonovaska-Trajkovska, Harris Gardner, Doug Holder, Sourav Sarkar, Erkut Tokman, Olena Jennings, Eileen Cleary, Rusty Barnes, Heather Sullivan, NilavroNill Shoovro, Zvi A. Sesling, Scott Thomas Outlar, John Patrick Robbins,

Kalpna Singh-Chitnis, William Walsh, and Jonathan Locke Hart.

Thank you to my dear friends, Jane Gregorich, Carol Schmidt, Sandy Shipp and Shirley Prescott in Illinois for their friendship and inspiration.

So many reading venues and festivals in the US and abroad have been so supportive these past years, always giving me a place to share my poetry. Too many to list but you know who you are. Thank you!

Thanks to my family: Dad, Kellis, Richard, and Alexander who are just the best!

A huge thank you to my partner William J. Kelle for everything. I am so appreciative of your support.

You keep me going!

About the Author

Gloria Mindock is editor of Červená Barva Press. She is an award-winning author of six poetry collections and three chapbooks. Her poems have been published and translated into eleven languages. Her recent book, *Ash*, was translated into Serbian by Milutin Durickovic and published by Alma Press in Belgrade in 2022. *Ash*, published by Glass Lyre Press (2021), won the International Impact Award, the NYC Big Book Award, the Firebird Speak Up Talk Radio Award, The Pacific Book Award, the International Award - The Princess, Noble Poetry Skills, Art Club of Ragkonik in Smederevo, Serbia, a Distinguished Favorite for the Independent Book Award, and a Bronze Medal from the North American Book Award. Other awards include the Allen Ginsburg Award for Community Service by the Newton Publishing Center, the Ibbetson Lifetime Achievement Award, the 5th and 40th Moon Prize from Writing in a Woman's Voice, numerous Pushcart nominations and three citations for Červená Barva Press as an editor and community service from the MA House of Representatives.

Gloria's work recently has appeared in *Gargoyle, The James Dickey Review, 10 x 10, Ibbetson, Growth: Journal of Literature, Culture, & Art (Macedonia), KGB Lit*, and others. Gloria was the Poet Laureate in Somerville, MA in 2017 & 2018. For more information about Gloria Mindock, visit her website at: www.gloriamindock.com

Author's Note

I stand with Ukraine. All my friends, throughout the world, stand with Ukraine.

In my poem "Bandages," I write of flowers being in a boot. I wish I could give credit for such a powerful image but I do not remember what book it was in.

Glass Lyre Press

exceptional works to replenish the spirit

Glass Lyre Press is an independent literary publisher interested in technically accomplished, stylistically distinct, and original work. Glass Lyre seeks diverse writers that possess a dynamic aesthetic and an ability to emotionally and intellectually engage a wide audience of readers.

Glass Lyre's vision is to connect the world through language and art. We hope to expand the scope of poetry and short fiction for the general reader through exceptionally well-written books, which evoke emotion, provide insight, and resonate with the human spirit.

Poetry Collections
Poetry Chapbooks
Select Short & Flash Fiction
Anthologies

www.GlassLyrePress.com

www.ingramcontent.com/pod-product-compliance
Lightning Source LLC
LaVergne TN
LVHW041627070526
838199LV00052B/3275